Heroes for Young Readers

Written by Renee Taft Meloche
Illustrated by Bryan Pollard

Adoniram Judson	Gladys Aylward
Amy Carmichael	Hudson Taylor
Betty Greene	Ida Scudder
Brother Andrew	Jim Elliot
Cameron Townsend	Jonathan Goforth
Corrie ten Boom	Loren Cunningham
C. S. Lewis	Lottie Moon
David Livingstone	Mary Slessor
Eric Liddell	Nate Saint
George Müller	William Carey

Heroes of History for Young Readers

Written by Renee Taft Meloche
Illustrated by Bryan Pollard

Daniel Boone
Clara Barton
George Washington
George Washington Carver
Meriwether Lewis

...and more coming soon

*Heroes for Young Readers Activity Guides and audio CDs
are now available! See the back of this book for more information.*

For a free catalog of books and materials contact
YWAM Publishing, P.O. Box 55787, Seattle, WA 98155
1-800-922-2143 www.ywampublishing.com

HEROES FOR YOUNG READERS

JIM ELLIOT

A Light for God

Written by Renee Taft Meloche
Illustrated by Bryan Pollard

YWAM
PUBLISHING
P.O. BOX 55787 SEATTLE, WA 98155

Jim Elliot: A Light for God   Text © 2004 by Renee Taft Meloche   Illustrations © 2004 by Bryan Pollard
Published by YWAM Publishing, P.O. Box 55787, Seattle, WA 98155   ISBN 978-1-57658-235-0   Printed in China.   All rights reserved.

A young boy named Jim Elliot
    just loved to be outdoors.
In Oregon, where he grew up,
    he camped, fished, and explored.

Like others in the nineteen thirties,
    he possessed few things,
but trips into the wilderness
    were richly challenging.

Jim's parents let him take these trips
    with other boys he knew
so he could learn resourcefulness
    and independence, too.

When Jim was home, his father, an
    evangelist, would read
him stories of brave people who
    risked much for those in need.

These Bible heroes—Moses, David,
    Esther—had refused
to live dull, cautious lives, the kind
    Jim also would not choose.

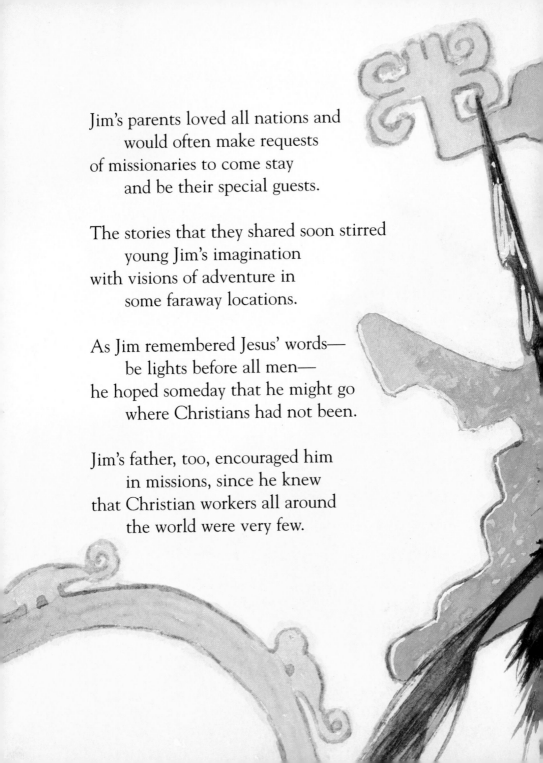

Jim's parents loved all nations and
would often make requests
of missionaries to come stay
and be their special guests.

The stories that they shared soon stirred
young Jim's imagination
with visions of adventure in
some faraway locations.

As Jim remembered Jesus' words—
be lights before all men—
he hoped someday that he might go
where Christians had not been.

Jim's father, too, encouraged him
in missions, since he knew
that Christian workers all around
the world were very few.

Jim did not hide his light in school.
    No one could overlook
his Bible, which he stacked on top
    of all his other books.

He went to Bible school, and soon
    he knew with certainty
that South America was where
    God wanted him to be.

Jim prayed, *Make me Your flame, O God—*
    a flame that will burn bright—
so people that I meet will hear
    of Your great love and light.

And so in nineteen fifty-two
    Jim sailed to Ecuador.
He studied Spanish in a town
    called Quito, near the shore.

He learned some basic health care, and
    quite soon the day arrived
to fly into the jungle and
    to share the Indians' lives.

A friend named Pete went with him, and
 they headed off with Nate,
a missionary pilot—
 experienced and first-rate.

The plane touched down some distance from
 the place where they would be
among a gentle Indian tribe
 who lived quite peacefully.

Then Jim and Pete began a long
    but fascinating trek.
They saw brightly colored butterflies
    and scary, large insects.

Huge kapok trees stood high above.
    Bright birds made squawking sounds.
As monkeys swung from tree to tree,
    snakes slithered on the ground.

A Christian worker welcomed them
    to their new destination.
He ran a boys' school and a clinic
    at his mission station.

They soon would learn to do the work
    this fine man had begun—
to teach the children, help the sick—
    since his time there was done.

The Indians came and very warmly
    greeted Jim and Pete,
and as good hosts served avocado
    and papaya treats.

To be good guests both Jim and Pete
    immediately learned
with grace to stomach swallowing
    some big fat chonta worms.

Jim learned the tribal language and
    worked hard with Pete, as planned,
to clear an airstrip so that Nate
    could soon securely land.

Weeks later, Nate's plane landed in
    a safe and smoothed-out spot.
With joy the Indians helped unload
    the goods that he had brought.

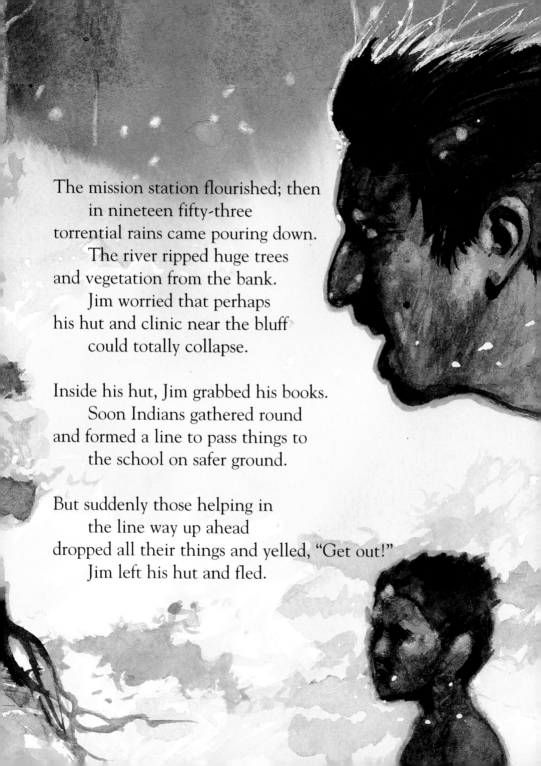

The mission station flourished; then
        in nineteen fifty-three
torrential rains came pouring down.
        The river ripped huge trees
and vegetation from the bank.
        Jim worried that perhaps
his hut and clinic near the bluff
        could totally collapse.

Inside his hut, Jim grabbed his books.
        Soon Indians gathered round
and formed a line to pass things to
        the school on safer ground.

But suddenly those helping in
        the line way up ahead
dropped all their things and yelled, "Get out!"
        Jim left his hut and fled.

He reached a clearing as a sudden
    crashing pierced his ears.
He turned and saw his hut roll down
    the bluff, then disappear.

The jungle shook again after
    an even bigger roar,
and Jim knew that it meant one thing:
    their clinic was no more.

It too had slipped into the raging
    river, and he feared
that he might lose the schoolhouse next,
    the rain was so severe.

The Indians once again helped Jim
    and Pete move what they'd stored
inside the school to places safer,
    farther from the shore.

They all worked hard till Jim and Pete,
    exhausted from the day,
were both invited to an Indian's
    hut that night to stay.

By early morning, things were worse
    and Jim could only stare.
Part of the airstrip and the school
    were just no longer there.

A whole year's work that they had done
    had all been washed away.
The two men stood in silence; there
    was nothing they could say.

While their bright flame was somewhat dimmed,
        the two men had no doubt—
they would not quit, they would rebuild.
        Their light would not burn out.

Soon clinics, schools, and churches in
        the villages nearby
were being built as well to serve
        the Indians in those tribes.

Jim missed a friend from Bible school,
    another missionary.
It was not long before he asked
    if she would like to marry.

Her name was Betty, and as soon
    as she became his bride,
she learned the tribal language too
    and they worked side by side.

And after sixteen months passed by
    they both were proud to be
the parents of a baby girl.
    They named her Valerie.

Just east of them were Indians called
    the Aucas, who were feared.
They lived deep in the jungle, killing
    those who ventured near.

Jim knew the reason that they killed:
    in past years they had known
white hunters who'd enslaved them and
    had burned down their small homes.

And no one knew just where they lived
    till one day Nate discovered
from in his Piper Cruiser plane
    their village home, uncovered.

Jim wondered if their anger from
    injustice in the past
could be replaced by Christian love,
    if shown to them at last.

He strongly felt that he should try
    to reach out with his life.
If just one Auca could know God,
    the risk was worth the price.

In January nineteen fifty-six,
    Jim, Nate, and Pete,
and two more men flew near the Aucas,
    landing on a beach.

And when they could, they radioed
    back to their wives to say
three Aucas had befriended them
    and then had gone away.

They sent a second message later,
    on another day,
reporting that more Aucas at
    that time were on their way.

They promised then to call again
    to keep their wives from worry.
They'd call that very afternoon—
    later, at four-thirty.

Back home, as Betty watched the clock,
    its hands crept slowly past
the time the call was due to come
    till darkness fell at last.

She felt a growing apprehension
    through the anxious night.
When no news came by morning, she
    knew something was not right.

A military rescue team
    and other people went
to search for them by helicopter.
    Soon more planes were sent.

But after four long days had passed,
    the news the women feared
was then confirmed: their husbands had
    been killed by Auca spears.

The news went all around the world
    about these five brave men
who gave their lives to spread God's Word.
    But this was not the end.

For Betty did not hate the Aucas,
    but instead she prayed
for them to know God and accept
    His loving Son someday.

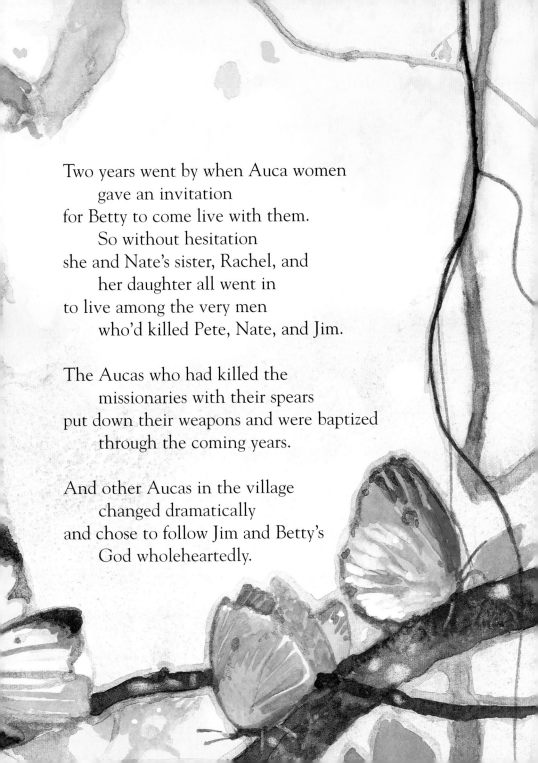

Two years went by when Auca women
        gave an invitation
for Betty to come live with them.
        So without hesitation
she and Nate's sister, Rachel, and
        her daughter all went in
to live among the very men
        who'd killed Pete, Nate, and Jim.

The Aucas who had killed the
        missionaries with their spears
put down their weapons and were baptized
        through the coming years.

And other Aucas in the village
        changed dramatically
and chose to follow Jim and Betty's
        God wholeheartedly.

Although Jim Elliot's life was short,
    his flame has never died,
for he ignited others to
    spread God's great love worldwide.

Like Jim we all can make a difference
    in our own lifetime.
If we love God and others too,
    our lights will brightly shine.

Christian Heroes: Then & Now

by Janet and Geoff Benge

Heroes for Young Readers and Heroes of History for Young Readers are based on the Christian Heroes: Then & Now and Heroes of History biographies by Janet and Geoff Benge. Don't miss out on these exciting, true adventures for ages ten and up!

Continued on the next page...

Heroes of History
by Janet and Geoff Benge

Abraham Lincoln: A New Birth of Freedom
Alan Shepard: Higher and Faster
Benjamin Franklin: Live Wire
Christopher Columbus: Across the Ocean Sea
Clara Barton: Courage under Fire
Daniel Boone: Frontiersman
Douglas MacArthur: What Greater Honor
George Washington Carver: From Slave to Scientist
George Washington: True Patriot
Harriet Tubman: Freedombound
John Adams: Independence Forever
John Smith: A Foothold in the New World
Laura Ingalls Wilder: A Storybook Life
Meriwether Lewis: Off the Edge of the Map
Orville Wright: The Flyer
Ronald Reagan: Destiny at His Side
Theodore Roosevelt: An American Original
Thomas Edison: Inspiration and Hard Work
William Penn: Liberty and Justice for All

...and more coming soon. Unit Study Curriculum Guides are also available.

Heroes for Young Readers Activity Guides
Educational and Character-Building Lessons for Children
by Renee Taft Meloche

Heroes for Young Readers Activity Guide for Books 1–4
Gladys Aylward, Eric Liddell, Nate Saint, George Müller

Heroes for Young Readers Activity Guide for Books 5–8
Amy Carmichael, Corrie ten Boom, Mary Slessor, William Carey

Heroes for Young Readers Activity Guide for Books 9–12
Betty Greene, David Livingstone, Adoniram Judson, Hudson Taylor

Heroes for Young Readers Activity Guide for Books 13–16
Jim Elliot, Cameron Townsend, Jonathan Goforth, Lottie Moon
Heroes of History for Young Readers Activity Guide for Books 1–4
George Washington Carver, Meriwether Lewis, George Washington, Clara Barton

Designed to accompany the vibrant Heroes for Young Readers books, these fun-filled Activity Guides lead young children through a variety of character-building and educational activities. Pick and choose from the activities or follow the included thirteen-week syllabus. An audio CD with book readings, songs, and fun activity tracks is available for each Activity Guide.

For a free catalog of books and materials contact
YWAM Publishing, P.O. Box 55787, Seattle, WA 98155
1-800-922-2143 www.ywampublishing.com